Presented to

Occasion

Happy Birthday

Date

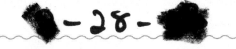
— 28 —

from: Aunty Michelle

Other books by Jackie Kendall

The Mentoring Mom: 11 Ways to Model Christ for Your Child

Say Goodbye to Shame: And 77 Other Stories of Hope and Encouragement

A Man Worth Waiting For: How to Avoid a Bozo

Free Yourself to Love: The Liberating Power of Forgiveness

In the Lady in Waiting Series

The Young Lady in Waiting: Developing the Heart of a Princess
By Jackie Kendall and Debbie Jones

Lady in Waiting: Developing Your Love Relationships
By Jackie Kendall and Debbie Jones

Lady in Waiting: Devotional Journal and Study Guide
By Debbie Jones and Jackie Kendall

Dama En Espera (Spanish-language Lady in Waiting)
By Debbie Jones and Jackie Kendall

Lady in Waiting for Little Girls

Strengthening the Heart of Your Princess

by Jackie Kendall & Dede Kendall

NEW HOPE PUBLISHERS

BIRMINGHAM, ALABAMA

New Hope* Publishers
P. O. Box 12065
Birmingham, AL 35202-2065
www.newhopepublishers.com

New Hope Publishers is a division of WMU*.

Library of Congress Cataloging-in-Publication Data

Kendall, Jackie.
Lady in waiting for little girls: strengthening the heart of your princess / Jackie Kendall and Dede Kendall.
      p. cm.
ISBN-13: 978-1-59669-265-7 (sc)
ISBN-10: 1-59669-265-0 (sc)
1. Mothers and daughters — Religious aspects — Christianity. 2. Daughters — Religious life. 3. Girls — Religious life. I. Kendall,
Dede. II. Title.
BV4529.18.K44 2009
248.8'45 — dc22
      2009016581

Interior Design: Glynese Northam

ISBN-10: 1-59669-265-0
ISBN-13: 978-1-59669-265-7

N104314• 0909 • 7.5M1

Dedicated to our daughters
and their daughters
and moms and daughters everywhere

The princess comes into the palace in all her glory.
Her gown has gold threads running through it.
—PSALM 45:13

~~~~~~~~~

You did it: you changed wild lament
into whirling dance;
You ripped off my black mourning band
and decked me with wildflowers.
I'm about to burst with song;
I can't keep quiet about you.
God, my God,
I can't thank you enough.
—PSALM 30:11–12 (THE MESSAGE)

Contents

"The heart of the mother is the schoolroom of the child."
— HENRY WARD BEECHER

One good mother is worth a hundred schoolmasters."
— GEORGE HERBERT

Welcome to

Lady in Waiting for Little Girls

There are some truths only a loving mother — or at least a loving mother figure — can teach a daughter. That's the focus of *Lady in Waiting for Little Girls: Strengthening the Heart of Your Princess* — a mother's heart strengthening the heart of her little princess, teaching her the truth about making godly choices in life.

Delightfully illustrated and age-appropriate, this book is the much-awaited prequel to the best-selling *Lady in Waiting*. These lessons portray for little ladies in waiting the same character-strengthening qualities *Lady in Waiting* encourages women to develop.

Customized for mom and daughter's use together, you'll find this keepsake book equips you to translate godly qualities into "princess" language for little girls aged approximately five to nine years old.

As you and your daughter spend many memorable moments together, *Lady in Waiting for Little Girls* will help you strengthen the heart of your princess,

empowering her to comprehend, to respond, and to remember God's Word, and to make godly choices.

What God Says About Teaching Your Daughter

Lady in Waiting for Little Girls will help you and your daughter to love God and remember what He has said to us.

As you move through the lessons, follow the Holy Spirit's lead in your own heart. And remember these key Scriptures about teaching your daughter.

"The Lord is our God. The Lord is the one and only God. Love the Lord your God with all your heart and with all your soul. Love him with all your strength. The commandments I give you today must be in your hearts. Make sure your children learn them. Talk about them when you are at home. Talk about them when you walk along the road. Speak about them when you go to bed. And speak about them when you get up. Write them down and tie them on your hands as a reminder. Also tie them on your foreheads. Write them on the doorframes of your houses. Also write them on your gates" (Deuteronomy 6:4–9).

The Bible helps us to see that this lifelong journey of a love relationship with God, growing in His wisdom, clearly begins in childhood, but the fullness of understanding grows as we grow. God said of children, of the child Samuel, and of Jesus, respectively:

Train a child in the way [she] should go. When [she] is old [she] will not turn from it (PROVERBS 22:6).

The boy Samuel continued to grow stronger. He also became more and more pleasing to the Lord and to people (1 SAMUEL 2:26).

Jesus became wiser and stronger. He also became more and more pleasing to God and to people (LUKE 2:52).

Mothers have the privilege of passing on a godly heritage. With this book, you can grasp this privilege and have fun as you encourage your little girl to be all she can be for Jesus!

Use award stickers, points, special privileges, or anything else you like to recognize and to keep a record of your daughter's progress.

Revisit weekly lessons, Love Notes, record answers to prayers, and remind your daughter of how God is strengthening the heart of His princess.

Your Guide to *Lady in Waiting for Little Girls*

The Heart of a Princess Quiz

Please begin with The Heart of a Princess Quiz on page 17. Here, each godly quality has an associated Scripture and a relevant story that you can use to engage your daughter's attention. When you have read the story to or with your daughter, ask her to place herself in the

story and then to choose one of the responses to the specific situation. The choices she makes will begin her journey with you through the book's contents and learning.

Princess Choices and Activities

After the quiz are 10 lessons about choices — *Princess Choices* **—** in a practical and engaging format for your daughter and you to do together. Yes, you should *do* the lessons because your daughter is probably like most children who learn best by *doing*. As your daughter reads, or you and your daughter read her lesson and do activities, you'll also find *(italicized suggestions)* as well as messages of encouragement to you, mom, to help explain further how to use the content.

Each lesson section indicates the minimum time in which to do the activity (00), however, you can proceed at your own pace.

Each lesson's activities include a Tiara Truth, Story, Princess Portrait, Princess Pearls, Princess Power, Princess Prayer, and Princess Pledge. These are described in detail here. We suggest you explore one lesson at a time. Initially, you can cover a lesson in a week. This gives you time to complete one or more Princess Power activities and to look up most of the Bible verses found in the Princess Pearls section.

When you have completed all the lessons, you'll induct your daughter into the Heart of a Princess Club. You'll find instructions for this on page 125. You and your daughter will want to revisit this keepsake book's messages and recall the lessons learned as many times as you desire, and whenever an opportunity arises as your daughter grows.

Here's a more detailed look at the six ways you will explore each Princess Choice in each lesson.

1. Message to Mom, Tiara Truth with Story (5 minutes or more)

A Message to Mom comes before each meaningful Tiara Truth and the attention-getting companion story. Read by you and/or your daughter, it introduces your daughter to a godly character trait she can choose.

2. Princess Portrait (5 minutes or more)

This activity focuses on a biblical person who exemplifies the Tiara Truth. As you read to and with your daughter, engage her in the story and discuss the wise choice the biblical person made. Ask your daughter what wise choice she can make in her life. This activity will display to her not only what the character quality "looks like" in the Bible but also what this truth can look like when applied in her life.

3. Princess Pearls (10 minutes or more)

Spend time with your daughter "stringing a beautiful pearl necklace." Where will you get the pearls? Look up Bible verses together and read aloud the "pearls" of wisdom found only in God's Word. **Note:** Try to use an age-appropriate Bible version — one your young reader can comprehend. Help her locate Scripture in her Bible, and encourage her to underline or highlight the verses, to develop good Bible-study habits. God's Word will grow in and transform your daughter's heart!

4. Princess Power (15 minutes or more, depending on activity)
Hands-on activities reinforce the choice of godly character traits. Engaging in fun, meaningful activities with your daughter will allow you to spend significant and memorable time together. You can save additional activities, for whenever you revisit a particular Tiara Truth during a lesson, or for use during one of life's teachable moments. You'll want to note any items needed for the activities, such as certain craft materials, and gather those items in advance.

5. Princess Prayer (1 to 5 to 15 minutes or more)
Pray with your daughter, and help build prayer practices into her for life. Use the Princess Prayer provided as a guide to show your daughter how to talk to God personally about what she is learning from Him — and how to wait in silence before Him. And allow the Holy Spirit to guide her.

6. Princess Pledge (5 minutes or more)
A journaling exercise, this is an opportunity for your daughter to confirm her promise to make godly choices and to share the thoughts and emotions of her mind and heart. This encourages your daughter to think for herself and decide what she will do with the truth about the godly choice she has explored during the lesson activities.

At various points during the lesson, you will see italicized suggestions for enacting stories with movement. Use your imagination too! And don't forget to read the Love Notes written to you and your daughter that are interspersed throughout these lessons. Let's get started!

The Princess Waltzes with the King

*D*o you remember reading or seeing the story about Cinderella? In this fairy tale, there is one special moment when the prince finally dances a waltz around a ballroom with Cinderella, and she becomes his princess. *(Illustrate . . . "A waltz looks like this.")*

How many times have you danced with your daddy? How about your grand-daddy or an uncle? Have you danced with another adult who takes good care of you and loves you? Have you ever placed your feet atop their shoes and danced around the living room or another place? How did it feel? Did it make you feel a little bit like a princess?

Do you know that a little girl's devotion and love for God is like a princess dancing with her king? The Bible explains it to us with these words, *"For all who are led by the Spirit of God are children of God"* (Romans 8:14 NRSV). Being led by God's Spirit is being led by the heavenly Father. Like dancing with your feet on top of an adult's shoes. *(You can waltz with your daughter, with her feet atop yours.)*

It is letting Jesus, through the Holy Spirit, carry you along to the places He wants you to go and to the truths He wants you to know and the choices He wants you to have.

Maybe you remember playing the game "follow the leader." The Bible says, "Since we live by the Spirit, let us march in step with the Spirit" (Galatians 5:25). That means, follow the Leader, God! God has wonderful privileges — choices — especially for you. This book will help you understand many of these choices.

Love Note: Before you go to bed tonight, why not ask daddy or mommy if you could dance around the living room? Say that you want to follow Jesus closely. How close? Like a princess dancing with the King.

Another picture of how to keep in step with the Spirit is to understand that the Holy Spirit who lives inside us is like a "nudge" from within when it comes to showing us what to do. This can be described as a holy nudge! The holy nudge is a wonderful reminder inside our heart, reminding us of what Jesus wants us to do; the choices He wants us to make. It's like He is a friend teaching us how to dance with Him — to keep step with Him in this dance of life. He reminds us of the dance steps . . . one-two-three, one-two- three . . . almost like a gliding waltz. **(Demonstrate waltz again.)**

The Bible tells us, "But the Father will send the Friend in my name to help you. The Friend is the Holy Spirit. He will teach you all things. He will remind you of everything I have said to you" (John 14:26).

Love Note to Mom: This book will be like a continual dance lesson. Because, when your daughter knows the King, she can follow Him her whole life.

Introduction

The Heart of a Princess Quiz
The Bad-Day Dress

When Dede was a little girl, her mommy bought her a back-to-school dress. The dress was made from green plaid. Yes, green plaid, with lots of little squares of green and black. Plaid cloth can be very pretty. But, honestly, Dede didn't like the green plaid dress at all!

One morning, as Dede was getting dressed for school, her mother wanted Dede to wear that green plaid dress. Well, Dede told her mom she simply couldn't wear that dress. She said she *knew* she would have a bad day if she wore the green plaid dress.

You may be wondering, *where on earth did Dede get that idea?* Well, Dede was remembering the *last* time she wore that green plaid dress. Some girls made fun of her — all because the dress was green plaid! The laughing girls acted unkind. Those girls were looking at a green plaid dress *they* didn't like. They were not even thinking about Dede's kind and loving heart. Those girls did not see what was inside Dede's heart!

Sadly, people can sometimes behave very unkind. *But,* it is a good thing for us that *God sees people differently.* Even though people look at what others look

like on the outside, God looks *into* the heart. The Bible, God's Word, says: "I do not look at the things people look at. Man looks at how someone appears on the outside. But I look at what is in the heart" (1 Samuel 16:7). That means that God sees our very thoughts!

This means God knows what we think *and* what we have a mind to do. You are His princess, but do you have the heart of a princess? True beauty comes from *inside*. It comes from the choices we make in our heart. True beauty does *not* come from pretty clothes or the style of our hair. True beauty shows when our thoughts — what we have a mind to *do* — are pleasing to God. We want our hearts to be as beautiful as our outside appearance. So let's take a look at what we have a mind to do with the following activity in our book. Let's discover if you have the heart God wants you to have — the heart of a princess.

What Makes A Princess?

Heart of a Princess Quiz

Introduce the quiz by telling your daughter that she will be making a choice in each of the situations you read together. Involve her in making the actual choice, based on what she thinks the Scripture says. Encourage her to tell you why her choice pleases the Lord. As your daughter works through the quiz, remind her that her heavenly Father is pleased when she makes wise and godly choices!

This activity will help your daughter understand that, when her heavenly Father looks at her, it's who she is on the inside that counts! Explain to her that He wants her to grow in this understanding, even though she may not always make all the right choices. He loves her!

Mom, read the following section to your daughter:

Princess,

Let's take a look at your princess privileges. As God's little princess, you have a right to choose what is best. By doing the following activity with my help, you'll discover the choices a true princess makes. You will see if you're making the choices God wants you to make. For each of the following situations, you get to make one of two choices. See if you have the heart of a princess—a heart to do what God thinks is best for His princess to do.

First, read the Tiara Truth with me. These are truths based on God's Word (the Bible). Think about what God's Word says. *(Give her time to think and to ask you to help her understanding as needed.)*

Then, read the question and the choices. You can then choose one answer by coloring in the circle ⟳ next to the answer you choose.

Tiara Truth: Obedience — Proverbs 1:8-9

"Listen to your father's advice. Don't turn away from your mother's teaching. What they teach you will be like a beautiful crown on your head. It will be like a chain to decorate your neck."

When your parents tell you it's time to put away your toys and wash your hands for dinner, what choice do you make? (Choose one.)
○ **I pretend I didn't hear, and keep playing with my toys.**
○ **I listen and obey right away and with a happy heart.**

Tiara Truth: Patience — Psalm 37:7

"Be still. Be patient. Wait for the Lord to act."

When your mom is talking on the phone and you want her to look at and listen to you, what choice do you make?
○ **I wait quietly for her to get off the phone. When mom is ready, I enjoy the privilege of her paying attention to me.**
○ **I whine, cry, or get upset because I must wait.**

Tiara Truth: Diligence — Proverbs 3:3

"Don't let love and truth ever leave you. Tie them around your neck. Write them on the tablet of your heart."

Your teacher sends home a note announcing that your school will be collecting toys for needy children. What choice do you make?

○ **I can't wait to get home and show Mom the note so we can start shopping for a special toy.**

○ **I start playing when I get home and forget all about the needy children.**

Tiara Truth: Inner Beauty
(being pretty on the inside) — 1 Peter 3:3–4

"[Fixing] your hair doesn't make you beautiful. Wearing gold jewelry or fine clothes doesn't make you beautiful. Instead, your beauty comes from inside you. It is the beauty of a gentle and quiet spirit. Beauty like that doesn't fade away. God places great value on it."

Some boys are teasing your friend about her haircut. You say:

○ **"I think you still look beautiful."** You enjoy the privilege of knowing what true beauty is.

○ **"Yeah, it looks like your hair was cut with a weed whacker!"**

Tiara Truth: Faith — Deuteronomy 31:6

"Be strong and brave. Don't be afraid of them and don't be frightened, because the LORD your God will go with you. He will not leave you or forget you" (NCV).

Your parents tell you that you're going to a new school in August. You choose to:

○ be a little nervous about going to a new school, but decide to not be afraid. You remember that God is with you. It's a privilege to trust in your heavenly Father.

○ have a temper tantrum and refuse to get out of the car on the first day of school.

Tiara Truth: Forgiveness — Ephesians 4:32

"Be kind and tender to one another. Forgive each other, just as God forgave you because of what Christ has done."

Your friend says she is not your friend anymore. You want to say something mean and hurtful. You choose to:

○ **Tell her that what she said hurt your feelings. You have the privilege of being a big girl who can forgive. You tell your mom so she can help you with those hurt feelings.**

○ **Tell all the girls in your class not to play with her during recess.**

Tiara Truth: LOVE — John 13:34

"Love one another, just as I have loved you."

For the Valentine's Day party, a classmate brings in goodie bags for everyone in the class. But, when all the bags are handed out, there is one girl who did not get one, and she starts to cry. You choose to:

○ **Say: "Don't be sad, I'll share my goodie bag with you." You enjoy the privilege of sharing with others and sharing God's love.**

○ **Turn and walk away pretending you did not see her.**

Tiara Truth: Contentment — Philippians 4:11

"I have learned to be content no matter what happens to me."

Your best friend gets the precious puppy you've been wanting for months. What choice do you make?

○ **Squeal with delight and celebrate with my friend.**

○ **Say something like, "That's not fair; that's the puppy I wanted!"**

~~~~~~~~~~~

Mom, continue reading the following section to your daughter:

So Princess, how did you do? You did super with most *(many, or some)* of your choices.

Let's now look at making these truths become more a part of your life as a little princess every day. These truths will guide your heart and bless your life as you grow. Before we begin, here is a special prayer written with you in mind.

Princess Prayer

Dear Father,

I pray that You would give *(Say your child's name here and as directed in the following sentences.)* the heart of a princess. Thank You, Jesus, for loving *(name)* with a forever love. May *(name)* always know and be secure in Your love.

♥ Help *(name)* to be content and happy with what she has been given.

♥ Help *(name)* to obey and learn from her parents, so that she can be crowned with honor.

♥ Create the pearl of patience in *(name)*'s heart as she learns to wait patiently.

♥ Wrap compassion and kindness around *(name)*'s heart.

♥ Help *(name)* to remember that true beauty comes from within.

♥ May *(name)* be strong and courageous, because she knows You are always with her.

♥ Help *(name)* to always give the gift of forgiveness.

♥ May *(name)* remember to love others as Jesus loves them!

(Say this together.) In Jesus's name, I pray. Amen.

Princess Choice 1 —

Obedience:
Surrendering to God

*D*ear Mom: This Tiara Truth of obedience will focus on the importance of obedience—your daughter choosing to obey her heavenly Father and yield to His perfect will. Of course, this includes your daughter obeying those whom God has placed in authority over her. She will begin to understand that He knows what's best for her. This lesson will probably be a wonderful reminder for you, too, to listen daily for the holy nudges toward obedience and surrender to God.

Message to Mom

How often have we mothers sensed that Jesus wants us to do something specific, yet ignored the holy nudge because we were too busy? Do we moms obey Jesus as quickly as we want our children to obey us? This is a question each of us must answer honestly.

> "Obedience makes every moment precious."
> —BROTHER ANDREW

Tiara Truth — Obedience

 This Tiara Truth of *obedience* will focus on the importance of obeying our heavenly Father and yielding to His perfect will. We will begin to understand that He knows what is best for us.

Obedience is saying a big yes to God. It is being quick to say, "Whatever, Lord God!" (in a good way). A princess is not afraid to say yes to Jesus. She does not insist on having her own way. She wants to surrender to God.

> "'Nothing is impossible with God. I serve the Lord,'" Mary answered. "May it happen to me just as you said it would'"
> (LUKE 1:37–38).

Mmm, What's That Smell?

Ask your daughter the following: What do you love to smell? I bet you love to smell chocolate chip cookies baking in the oven or maybe you love the yummy smell of brownies! ***(Possibly have a favorite baked good available.)*** Did you know that you have your own special smell?

A little girl named Alexandra loved her mom's special smell. Whenever her mom went out of town to teach others about Jesus, Alexandra would go in her mom's closet and smell her mom's clothes. Her mom's sweet smell made Alexandra's heart happy.

A little boy named Austin loves to smell his grandpa's head! He loves to climb on his grandpa's back so he can sniff his head. Does Austin sniffing his grandpa's head sound pretty silly? Do you have someone you like to hug and to sniff her neck?

Listen to this story about Dede and a special smell. One morning, Dede was running around, getting ready to leave the house in a big rush. She grabbed her favorite bottle of perfume from the dresser as she hurried to the front door. But in her hurry, Dede let the perfume bottle slip right out of her hand, and it smashed onto the tile floor! The beautiful bottle shattered into pieces, and the expensive perfume spilled all over. Not having time to clean up the mess, Dede had to leave the broken glass and puddle of perfume to clean up a short time later.

When Dede came home that evening, she thought about her pretty perfume bottle, broken and all over the floor. She walked sadly toward the front door and slowly turned the handle.

But what do you think greeted Dede when she opened the door? You are right! She was met with the most wonderful smell. Better than chocolate chip cookies! The room was filled with the sweet smell of her very favorite perfume! The bottle had been broken and the perfume had poured out.

Discuss with your daughter.

Do you know that this is what happens when we say yes to Jesus? Every time we say yes to Jesus and obey Him — even if it feels like we are being broken — our life becomes a sweet perfume or gift that we get to give Jesus! You know what? I think that's when the Lord says, "Mmm, what's that wonderful smell? Oh, I know what that is, that must be my precious princess obeying me again!" Obedience is the best gift that we can give Jesus!

When we choose to obey our parents quickly, we are making the wise choice with the heart of a princess. Sometimes we may not make the wise choice to obey quickly; we may demand our own way. When we disobey our parents . . . oops . . . someone needs a Tiara Time Out!

Read the following Bible story with your daughter.

"Nothing is impossible with God." That's what an angel told the young girl Mary.

Young Mary chose to respond to God in this way: "I serve the Lord." Mary answered, "May it happen to me just as you said it would." Then the angel left her. Mary knew it was a privilege to obey her heavenly Father in this way.

Do you remember the Christmas story about this young girl named Mary, to whom an angel appeared? Mary was given the privilege to carry the Son of God and become His mommy. Mary was an amazing girl, obedient and full of trust in her heavenly Father. Did you know that God is looking for girls who are eager to obey and trust Him? Are you ready to stand up and shout, "Whatever, Lord!"? The Bible tells us more about Mary.

In Nazareth there lived a young woman named Mary. Mary was engaged to marry a man named Joseph. Joseph was the great-great-great-great-great grandson of King David. One day God sent the angel Gabriel to Nazareth to visit Mary. When Mary saw the shining angel standing there, Mary was very frightened. But Gabriel said, "Do not be afraid, Mary, for you have found favor with God. *(Tell your daughter that means that God was very happy with Mary.)* You will give birth to a son, and you shall call him Jesus."

Confused and disturbed, Mary tried to think what the angel could mean. Gabriel said to her, "The Holy Spirit will come upon you, and the power of the Most High will overshadow you. The

child to be born will be called holy, the Son of God." And Mary said, "I am God's servant, whatever God says, I will do." *(Adapted from Matthew 1:18–25 and Luke 1:26–38.)*

Mary could have said no to the angel. But she said yes. Mary was a wise girl who put God first. She let everything happen the way God wanted!

Discuss with your daughter: How could a little girl have grown into such a trusting teen as Mary? How did young Mary move from fear to faith when the angel said she would have a child? One of the reasons is that Mary had the heart of a princess. She learned as a little girl how to obey her mom and dad. Her obedience as a little girl prepared her to say yes to God's will for her as a teenager. A princess knows the Tiara Truth of *obedience*, the wisest choice a princess can make, is to shout a big yes to God: "Yes and whatever, LORD!" (See Luke 1:38).

Princess Pearls

Now it's time for you and your daughter to string a beautiful "pearl necklace." Where will you get the pearls for this necklace? Together, read aloud the pearls of wisdom found in God's Word. Each verse is like a beautiful pearl. Have your daughter underline or highlight the verse in her Bible. Answer questions she has about the Word as the Holy Spirit leads you. This a great way for her to develop a good Bible study habit. May the precious pearls of God's Word transform your daughter's heart into the heart of a princess.

Mary chose obedience. These Bible words show us that we should choose obedience.

Luke 1:38 "I serve the Lord," Mary answered. "May it happen to me just as you said it would."

Ruth 1:16 "But Ruth replied, 'Don't try to make me leave you and go back. Where you go I'll go. Where you stay I'll stay. Your people will be my people. Your God will be my God.'" Ruth's Princess Choice was surrender, obedience to God.

Proverbs 1:8–9 "Listen to your father's advice. Don't turn away from your mother's teaching. What they teach you will be like a beautiful crown on your head. It will be like a chain to decorate your neck."

Proverbs 23:19 "My child, listen and be wise. Keep your heart on the right path."

Psalm 119:105 "Your word is like a lamp that shows me the way. It is like a light that guides me."

Matthew 5:3 "How happy are those who know their need for God." (Phillips)

Luke 1:38 "I belong to the Lord, body and soul . . . let it happen as you say." (Phillips)

Mark 14:3–9 A young woman gives her most precious treasure to Jesus." (paraphrased)

Psalm 73:28 "But it is good for me to draw near to God." (NKJV)

Help your daughter as needed to read the instructions. Allow her to do the activity on her own as much as possible. Please remind your daughter to never use a stove or a glue gun without your protection.

★ Write your own "Whatever, Lord" cheer. Grab some pompoms and shout it out! Give me a W-H-A-T-E-V-E-R! Perform your cheer for your family.

★ Mom-and-Me Time: Make a treasure box. Using a small gift box or an unfinished wood-hinged box purchased from a craft store, paint with acrylic paint and decorate it with jewels such as sequins and pearls.

★ Draw a picture of all your "wishes," and place the picture in your treasure box, giving your hopes and dreams to Jesus. As you place your pictures in the treasure box, you are saying to Jesus, "I trust You with all my hopes and dreams."

★ Mom-and-Me Time: Bake a cake and frost it. Place a candle on the cake for every wish (hope and dream) you have . . . when you blow out the candles, give those wishes to Jesus!

★ Boil an Egg! With Mom's help, put an egg in a pot of water. Bring it to a boil. Boil the egg for about ten minutes. What happened to the egg? That's right, it got hard.

When you disobey your parents or the Lord, your heart becomes hardened just like that boiled egg! When you obey, your heart remains tender. Jesus wants you to have a tender heart! Draw a picture of a time this week when you obeyed.

Princess Prayer

Dear Jesus,

I am so thankful for Your love. I place all my hopes, dreams, and wishes in Your hands, because I know that I can trust You. Help me to obey You each day and not to demand my own way. I give my princess heart to You.

In Jesus's name, I pray. Amen.

Princess Pledge

I promise to _____

~~~~~~

~~~~~~

~~~~~~

~~~~~~

~~~~~~

~~~~~~

~~~~~~

~~~~~~

~~~~~~

~~~~~~

~~~~~~

Diligence:
Showing God's Love

This Tiara Truth of diligence will focus on the many ways and opportunities your daughter can serve the Lord by serving others.

Message to Mom

Does your daughter see you willingly volunteering to serve those in your family, church, and community? The good deeds we do for others in Jesus's name are the best ways to be a witness for Him.

> "We love God best when we love each other well."
> — STEVEN CURTIS CHAPMAN

Tiara Truth — Diligence

 Don't you love being wrapped up in a big fluffy towel when you have finished your bath? Maybe you love to wrap up with a comfy, cozy blanket on a chilly day. *(Wrap in a favorite blanket for the story time.)* Did you know that God wants us to wrap kindness and compassion around our heart like a comfy blanket? When we show kindness and compassion, we have the heart of a princess.

When we are compassionate and kind to others, this means we have a servant's heart. The wise princess knows she is the happiest and most full of joy when she is diligent and doing something important for someone else! Princess, you can make a difference! You can help a discouraged (sad) friend by praying for her and by making her a pretty card.

Make sure your princess heart is a servant's heart and find a way to do something for someone else!

> *"Don't let love and truth ever leave you. Tie them around your neck. Write them on the tablet of your heart. Then you will find favor and a good name in the eyes of God and people"*
> (PROVERBS 3:3–4).

Banana Nerds and Red Licorice

Jessica's third-grade class was taking up a collection of needed items to send to a missionary family in Japan. Two suggested items captured third-grader Jessica's tender heart. The items were banana nerds and red licorice! Jessica came home and pleaded with her mom to go find these items so she could send them to Japan. As her mom was leaving for the store, Jessica yelled, "If you can't find the nerds, please get an extra large package of red licorice."

Even an eight-year-old girl can show her concern for those serving others in foreign countries. She showed her servant's heart by sending something she really enjoys, banana nerds and red licorice, to the missionary kids. Even a little girl can serve the King of the universe.

A nine-year-old girl who went on a missions trip was working among the poor. This little girl's name was Jessi. As Jessi was chatting with an older teenage girl one night, Jessi explained how Jessi became a Christian when she was only four-years-old. Because of Jessi's courage to talk about her love for Jesus, this older teenage girl gave her heart to Jesus that night! A little girl can lead a big girl to Jesus!

Love Note: Princess, you can make a difference for Jesus! A princess can show her compassion and kindness by helping others.

Princess Portrait — Rebekah

Princess, don't be a Sleeping Beauty waiting for a prince to kiss you awake. Jesus wants you to develop (grow) godly character. He will change you into the beautiful princess He created you to be.

Have you ever offered to do something you didn't have to do? Well, that is exactly what Rebekah did. Listen to Rebekah's story found in Genesis. Think about the beautiful and diligent Rebekah in this true story.

Rebekah went down to the spring of water. She filled her jar and came up again. The servant hurried to meet her. He said, "Please give me a little water from your jar."

"Have a drink, sir," she said. She quickly lowered the jar to her hands. And she gave him a drink. After she had given him a drink, she said, "I'll get water for your camels too. I'll keep doing it until they finish drinking." So she quickly emptied her jar into the stone tub. Then she ran back to the well to get more water. She got enough for all of his camels. The man didn't say a word. He watched her closely. He wanted to learn whether the Lord had given him success on the journey he had made. (See Genesis 24:16–21).

Genesis 24 describes Rebekah as a hard worker, carrying a jar on her shoulder and caring for her dad's sheep. Her respect for others showed through her kindness to a stranger in verse 18, "Certainly, sir," she said, and she quickly lowered the jug for him to drink.

Rebekah was not a lazy girl! She cared for the needs of others. Do you know what she did next? She offered to get water for the camels. Have you ever seen a camel? Can you imagine how many buckets of water those thirsty camels could drink? The Bible says, "So she quickly emptied the jug into the watering trough and ran down to the well again. She kept carrying water to the camels until they had finished drinking."

Discuss with your daughter: Rebekah decided to put someone else's needs ahead of her own. She shared the water and served without even being asked! When you decide to put someone else's needs ahead of your own, it's the best way to have a happy heart! When was the last time you helped your mom, or a sister, brother, or friend? When was the last time you were a helper at your school?

JOY works this way:
J= Jesus (first)
O= Others (second)
Y= You (last)

Princess Pearls

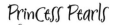

Don't forget to underline the precious pearls of God's Word in a Bible your little princess can read.

Ruth chose diligence. These Bible words show us that we should choose diligence.

Ruth 2:2 And Ruth the Moabitess said to Naomi, "Let me go to the fields and pick up the leftover grain behind anyone in whose eyes I find favor."

Naomi said to her, "Go ahead, my daughter" (NIV).

Hebrews 10:24 "Let us think about each other and help each other to show love and do good deeds" (NCV).

Hebrews 13:16 "Don't forget to do good. Don't forget to share with others. God is pleased with those kinds of offerings."

Ephesians 5:15–17 "So be very careful how you live. Do not live like people who aren't wise. Live like people who are wise. Make the most of every opportunity."

Isaiah 56:6–7 "They want to love me and worship me. They keep the Sabbath day and do not misuse it. And they are faithful in keeping my covenant. Then I will bring them to my holy mountain of Zion. I will give them joy in my house.

1 Corinthians 15:58 "Give yourselves completely to the work of the Lord."

Proverbs 11:25 "Anyone who renews others will be renewed."

Colossians 3:23 "Work at everything you do with all your heart. Work as if you were working for the Lord, not for human masters."

Princess Power — It's your turn!

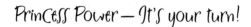

Have fun!

★ Ministry of Prayer: Mom-and-Me Time: Make a photo prayer journal and place pictures of your friends and family in a 4-by-6-inch album or larger. Use this journal as a reminder to pray for them. When God answers a prayer, thank Him for the answer and then write it on a praise list. Decorate the cover with foam craft material purchased from a craft store or materials Mom has at home.

★ Go on a Prayerwalk: Take a prayerwalk around your neighborhood. As you walk with your family members, pray for your neighbors, teachers, friends, and family. When you see toys in a yard, ask Jesus to bless the children who live in that house. Pray that they would see the love of Jesus in you!

★ Ministry of Helps: Mom-and-Me Time: Clean out your toy chest or closet and donate the toys and clothes you have outgrown or would just like to give to charity.

★ Ministry of Encouragement: Look around to see if any friends need cheering up.

★ Make a card or picture for someone who is sick using colored construction paper, decorative stickers, and markers.

★ Encourage a friend by helping her study for a test.

★ Make and decorate heart-shaped cookies. Share them with someone who needs cheering up! Remind them that you love them! And Jesus loves them too!

★ Ministry of Teaching: Share and read a story book with a younger child.

★ Teach a younger child how to tie his or her shoes.

★ Ministry of Service: Mom-and-Me Time: Do a missions project such as Operation Christmas Child, Angel Tree, or another project you choose to do in your neighborhood or elsewhere.

Princess Prayer

Dear Jesus,

Help me to be a wise girl and make the most of every chance to help others. I know you have made me for a Yourself, and I want to please you by serving You. Help me to not miss a chance to help someone this week.

In Jesus's name, I pray. Amen.

I promise to ~~~~~~

~~~~~~

~~~~~~

~~~~~~

~~~~~~

~~~~~~

~~~~~~

~~~~~~

~~~~~~

~~~~~~

~~~~~~

~~~~~~

Faith:
Being a Princess Warrior!

Dear Mom: This Tiara Truth of faith will focus on the impor- **Message** tance of knowing that God is always with us, and He wants us **to Mom** to know that we have nothing to fear, because He loves us. You will introduce the concept of being *full of faith* rather than *full of fear*: *Faith-full* instead of *fear-full*.

Do our daughters see us walking daily in peaceful trust or do they see us anxious and fearful? Did you know that anxiety has been defined as having a split mind? Is your mind split between doubts and wavering faith? Or are you faith-full too? God daily sends us faith-strengthening text messages through His Word but we too often have our phones turned off.

Tiara Truth — Faith

Be Princess Faith-full, full of faith, not afraid of what seems impossible. Faith means being sure of the things we hope for. And faith means knowing that something is real even if we do not see it.

Princess, put your faith and hope in God. He is the one who knows your future, and loves you enough to give you the very best! Are you more like "Princess Fear-full" or are you like "Princess Faith-full?"

"Without faith it isn't possible to please God" (HEBREWS 11:6).

Princess Fear-full Learns to be Princess Faith-full

There was a little girl who was so afraid of the dark that she couldn't go to sleep at night without a night light. Every night her mommy or daddy would pray with her and say out loud at the end of the prayer, *"God didn't give us a spirit that makes us weak and fearful. He gave us a spirit that gives us power and love. It helps us control ourselves"* (2 Timothy 1:7).

This shy, fearful little girl grew up to speak and sing in front of hundreds of people! She even acted in plays. Isn't that amazing? Although Jesus gave this princess the courage to get up and speak or sing in front of hundreds of people, she still sometimes struggles with fear.

This once fearful princess grew up to be a married lady who still must *choose* to trust God rather than fear. *"If you are afraid of people, it will trap you. But if you trust in the Lord, he will keep you safe"* (PROVERBS 29:25).

Love Note: Fear is not something that only affects little girls; even big girls struggle with fear. You can ask Mommy to tell you what she fears and how she prays that God will help her.

Princess Portrait — Deborah

There is no reason to fear when God is on your side. He can help you do great and mighty things! When I think of a courageous (brave) girl, I think of Deborah. Do you know who Deborah was in the Bible? Her story is in Judges 4 and 5.

Deborah was a leader in a place named Ephraim. Everyday, she would sit under a palm tree and the people would come to her for advice. At that time the children of Israel were in trouble. They were at war, and even though they had God on their side, all the people were afraid. All the people, except Deborah! So warrior Deborah led the army in battle, and do you know what happened? God gave them the victory! Deborah is proof that we can conquer *(explain meaning, to overcome)* our fears and face difficult situations, because God can help us do mighty things!

Deborah must have learned as a little girl to replace fear with faith in her great God. Why do I think that? Because Deborah grew up to be a woman who led soldiers into battle when the leader Barack was too afraid to lead by himself. Deborah led the way in battle. Deborah was a bold and brave woman. Even though a princess, one can be brave enough to be a warrior. Hey, you can be a Warrior Princess like Deborah!

Love Note: Discuss with your daughter her fears and how you and God can help her to overcome them.

May the precious pearls of God's Word transform your daughter's heart into the heart of a princess! (Don't forget to encourage your daughter to underline the precious pearls of God's Word in her Bible.)

Ruth 1:16 "But Ruth said, 'Don't try to make me leave you and go back. Where you go I'll go. Where you stay I'll stay. Your people will be my people. Your God will be my God.'"

Hebrews 11:1–3 Faith is being sure of what we hope for. It is being certain of what we do not see. That is what the people of long ago were praised for. We have faith. So we understand that everything was made when God commanded it. *(Read more in Hebrews 11, about all those who are described as "faithful." Many people call this Bible passage the Hall of Faith.)*

Romans 10:17 "So faith comes from hearing the message. And the message that is heard is the word of Christ."

1 Peter 5:7 "Turn all your worries over to him. He cares about you."

Romans 8:32 "God did not spare his own Son. He gave him up for us all. Then won't he also freely give us everything else?"

Deuteronomy 31:6 "Be strong and brave . . . the Lord your God will go with you" (NCV). You are a Princess Warrior!

Isaiah 41:10 "So do not be afraid . . . I will make you strong and help you."

Psalm 119:92 If I had not taken delight in your law, I would have died because of my suffering.

Ephesians 6:11 "Put on all of God's armor. Then you can stand firm against the devil's evil plans."

1 Thessalonians 5:18 "Give thanks no matter what happens. God wants you to thank him because you believe in Christ Jesus." **(*This is a princess battle song!*)**

Habakkuk 3:17–19 **(*This is a Princess battle song too!*)** "Though the fig tree does not bud and there are no grapes on the vines, though the olive crop fails and the fields produce no food, and though there are no sheep in the pen and no cattle in the stalls, yet I will rejoice in the Lord, I will be joyful in God my Savior. The Sovereign Lord is my strength; he makes my feet like the feet of a deer, he enables me to go on the heights" (NIV).

Have fun together!

★ What am I afraid of? I can talk to Mom about what scares me. I can draw a picture of a time when I was afraid. I'll title my picture: I WILL TRUST IN JESUS!

Love Note: Princess, if you are afraid, you can always pray to God and He will help you! Thank God for His awesome power to protect you from harm and for always being with you even when you are afraid.

★ Memorize Romans 10:17: "So faith comes from hearing the message. And the message that is heard is the word of Christ."

Love Note: Princess, spending time in God's Word is the best way to grow in your faith and become Princess Faith-full! Did you know that God's Word, the Bible, is like a sword? When we have God's Word in our heart that helps us not to sin and make wrong choices. So, Princess, grab your sword and tell Jesus: "I won't be afraid. I will trust in You, God!"

★ Decorate a pillowcase. Using fabric paint or a permanent marker, print the Bible verse on a pillowcase with Mom's help.

"For God has not given us a spirit of fear"
(2 Timothy 1:7 NKJV).

Love Note: Some junior high girls took their special pillowcases to camp. These pillowcases had their favorite Bible verse painted on them too.

Princess, don't be afraid, Jesus will give you His peace. Choose to trust God and not be Princess Fear-full! Sweet dreams, Princess Faith-full!

Dear Jesus,

Help me to trust and hope in You and not to be afraid. Thank You, God, for always protecting and caring for me. I want to be Princess Faith-full, not Princess Fear-full.

In Jesus's name, I pray. Amen!

Princess Pledge

I promise to

Princess Choice 4 —

Virtue:

Keeping Princess Lips

*D*ear Mom: This Tiara Truth of virtue will focus on the impor-   Message
tance of inner beauty. Discuss with your daughter the value   to Mom
of inner beauty as you examine the character qualities (kindness,
gentleness, honesty, and so on) that she can build in her life to be a truly beautiful
young lady.

Do our daughters see us always worried about our weight? Do daughters
see us on a steady diet of "mall therapy" to accentuate our exteriors? Do they see
us focusing more on our outer beauty than the lasting beauty of a godly heart?

Your child is a mirror of what fills the castle of your heart.

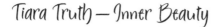

Tiara Truth — Inner Beauty

How do you know if a princess has inner beauty? Check out these beauty tips: Her words and her clothing show her beauty inside and out. Only sweet and uplifting words should flow from the mouth of a princess. Mom and daughter are both princesses, so their lips should be full of kindness (Proverbs 31:26. The lip gloss on their lips should be speaking the truth in love. (See Ephesians 4:15). Princess words should build up and encourage. *(Moisten your lips with clear gloss.)* Mean words should never come from the lips of a princess. Gossip, or "mean talk," hurts princess girlfriends. (See Proverbs 16:28).

> *"Your beauty should not come from outward adornment, such as braided hair and the wearing of gold jewelry and fine clothes. Instead, it should be that of your inner self, the unfading beauty of a gentle and quiet spirit, which is of great worth in God's sight"* (1 PETER 3:3 NIV).

Do you like to go shopping? Do you like to twirl around in the dressing room when you put on a pretty dress? I bet you are just like two little girls named Kenna and Kara! They love to twirl round and round in the dressing room when they put on a pretty pink or blue dress! *(Twirl in a circle with your daughter.)* It's fun to shop for new clothes. Listen to what a little girl learned about her clothing choices.

Kenna's Wise Fashion Choice

Kenna was only four-years-old when she began to understand what *appropriate* clothing (*acceptable clothing*) means. When she goes shopping with her grandmother, Kenna points out the tops that are too short and would show too much of her tummy. She is quick to say, "These tops are not appropriate." Her mommy wanted her to understand even at a young age what it means to make right choices in what she wears.

Did you know your body is God's house? Jesus lives there. Do you take care of His house? You can take care of His house by making wise choices not only with what you wear but also about what you say and do. Remember, a princess has clothing that reminds others that she is a princess for God.

Princess Portrait — Esther "More Than a Pretty Face"

A young girl wins a beauty contest and her inner beauty allows her to be chosen by the King of Persia!

Esther was one of the most beautiful girls in Persia. She entered a year-long beauty contest. The winner would be chosen as the next queen of the nation of Persia! Esther won the contest and found favor with the King. What is so amazing about Esther is, although her dad and mom both died when she was a little girl, she grew up to be a loving young woman. Her lips matched her pure heart; she was beautiful inside and out. There were many beautiful young women brought before the King, but Esther was chosen because she had the heart of a princess! (adapted from the Book of Esther)

Ruth 3:11 "And now, my daughter, don't be afraid. I will do for you all you ask. All my fellow townsmen know that you are a woman of noble character" (NIV).

See Genesis 24:16–25 Isaac was attracted to inner beauty . . . hard worker, pure, kind, and good character; cared for others, servant, attentive to others needs.

1 Corinthians 6:20 "Christ has paid the price for you. So use your bodies in a way that honors God."

Galatians 5:22–23 "The fruit of the Spirit is love, joy, peace, patience, kindness, goodness, faithfulness, gentleness and self-control" (NIV).

See 1 Samuel 16:7. The Lord looks at the heart.

Proverbs 31:30 Charm can fool you. Beauty fades. But a woman who has respect for the Lord should be praised.

Proverbs 4:20–23
   "My [daughter], pay attention to what I say.
   Listen closely to my words.
   Don't let them out of your sight.
   Keep them in your heart.

They are life to those who find them.
They are health to your whole body.
Above everything else, guard your heart.
It is where your life comes from."

Love Note on important princess beauty tips: Only sweet and uplifting words flow from the mouth of a princess. Mom and daughter are both princesses so their lips should be full of kindness (Proverbs 31 — law of kindness).

♥ The lip gloss on their lips should be speaking truth in love. (See Ephesians 4:15.)

♥ *Princess words build up, not tear down. (See Ephesians 4:29.)*

♥ *Mean words should never come from the lips of a princess. (Princess Lips and BFF [best friends forever]) (See Proverbs 17:17.)*

♥ *Gossip, "mean-girl talk," separates princess girl friends . . . gossip blocks BFF. (See Proverbs 16:28.)*

★ Make a collage of appropriate clothing choices. Cut out pictures from magazines and catalogs of appropriate clothing choices and glue the pictures onto poster board. This will be a super reminder as you get dressed in the morning. Are there clothes in your closet that are not appropriate? If you said yes, then it is time for a "clean sweep!" Ask Mom to help you with this task!

★ Using craft beads, make a necklace to remind you of the "pearls" of godly character qualities found in Galatians 5:22–23: love, joy, peace, patience, kindness, goodness, faithfulness, gentleness, and self-control.

Love Note: Princess, as these pearls develop, your life will become like a beautiful necklace of godly character.

★ Inside a large paper heart, write all the qualities you can think of that describe inner beauty. Mom may need to help if you are a younger princess.

(Galatians 5:22–23 is a wonderful verse to memorize that describes inner character!)

★ Make a paper BFF (Best Friends Forever) chain. Cut strips of construction paper 1 inch wide and 8 ½ inches long. Write the name of a friend and something special about that friend on the paper strip.

★ Make a paper ring and tape it closed. Keep making rings and connecting them until you have a friendship chain. Hang this special chain on your mirror as a reminder to thank the Lord for all the BFFs He has given you!

Princess Prayer

Dear Jesus,

I want to be known for having a beautiful heart. Help me to make appropriate and acceptable choices in what I wear and in what I do and say. May I have the true princess lips of kindness. I want to have the lasting beauty that comes from within.

In Jesus's name, I pray. Amen

Princess Pledge

I promise to

Princess Choice 4 — Virtue

Devotion:
Growing God's Love

*D*ear Mom: This Tiara Truth of devotion will focus on the   Message
importance of spending time with God, as your daughter reads   to Mom
His love letter, the Bible. Of course, the Bible is for our instruc-
tion, training in righteousness, and so much more, to perfect us as God desires
(2 Timothy 3:16). And as moms, we want to model the value of the love God
reveals to us. Do our daughters see us too busy to spend a few moments each day
with Jesus? Does your daughter know where your "quiet time" place is in your
home, where you keep your Bible and, possibly a journal?

"There is no lasting happiness, fulfillment or success apart from a
consistent, daily growing relationship with Jesus through His Word."
— M.E.CRAVENS

"The Word of God is shallow enough to not drown the young, but
deep enough that theologians will never touch the bottom."
— ANONYMOUS

Tiara Truth — Devotion

Did you know that God wants you to love Him with your whole heart? What does that mean? Think about how much you love your family. Now, that's a lot of love! God wants every girl (and boy) to learn about loving God as much as you love your family. God even wants you to love Him as much as your best friend or your precious pet.

> *"Love the Lord your God with all your heart, and with all your soul. Love him with all your strength" (Deuteronomy 6:5).*

One day some parents brought their children to see Jesus. The disciples (Jesus's close friends) didn't want the children to disturb the Master. But Jesus always had time for children. Jesus saw the little children, and immediately asked them to come close to Him. A girl with the heart of a princess would be the first to want to be blessed by Jesus. She would want to be the first one to sit with Him. *"Let the one the Lord loves rest safely in him. The Lord guards [her] all day long. The one the Lord loves rests in his arms"* (Deuteronomy 33:12).

Sweeter than Honey

Did you know that the teacher (Rabbi) in Bible times would pour honey on children's writing slates (small chalkboards)? Imagine what a mess children made with sweet, sticky, dripping honey? Why would a teacher allow such a messy treat? The teacher had a very important lesson about God's Word to teach students.

The teacher could say, "My child, lick the honey. Don't forget that God's words are sweet; more delicious than candy." (In Bible times they didn't have the candy we have. Honey was their candy.) The teacher would continue, "Taste, my child, and see that God is good!" Princess, taste some honey *(you may taste together)*. Remember, God says, "Your words are very sweet to my taste! They are sweeter than honey to me" (Psalm 119:103). Princess, that is how God wants you to feel about His Word, the Bible!

I know a little girl who wrote about the Bible in her journal when she was eight years old. She said, "God, I really like Your book." *(Show the Bible.)* She liked to write stories. She always included her love for God. One day, she wrote a story, "What I Want to Be." She wrote, "I love God . . . I love God . . ." ten times around the edge of her special journal. Princess, you can have a special journal too. You can write, "I love God, and I like His Bible."

Princess Portrait — Mary

Did you know there were three very special Mary's in Jesus' life? Of course, there was Jesus's mother, Mary. There also was a second Mary, who stayed near the Cross with Jesus's mother as He died (when most of His disciples ran away). That Mary also was the first to see Jesus after His resurrection. Then the third Mary, along with her sister, was a good friend to Jesus. He often ate at their house. This Mary loved sitting at His feet, learning more about God.

One day, this Mary's sister, Martha, got mad because Mary was sitting, listening to Jesus. Martha wanted Mary to help with food. Mary chose wisely to listen to Jesus instead. Mary always knew that listening to Jesus was the best way to spend her time.

Love Note: So Princess, how early can a girl walk with Jesus? How early can a heart be full of love for God? How old does a girl have to be to show others her devotion for God?

I know a seven-year-old prince, Josiah, who became king of Judah (2 Chronicles 24:1). At eight, he showed everyone his devotion to God. Do you know a little boy who shows others that he loves Jesus? Do you know a little girl who shows she loves Jesus? Decide to spend time reading His love letter, the Bible. Your love for Jesus will grow as you read His Word and pray. And you will begin to understand the wonderful plans He has for you!

Princess Pearls

May the precious pearls of God's Word transform your daughter's heart into the heart of a princess!

Ruth 1:12 "May the Lord reward your work, and your wages be full from the Lord, the God of Israel, under whose wings you have come to seek refuge."

Psalm 27:8 "My heart has heard you say, "Come and talk with me." And my heart responds, "Lord, I am coming" (NLT).

1 John 4:19 "We love because he first loved us."

Jeremiah 31:3b "I have loved you with a love that lasts forever."

Psalm 51:10 "God, create a pure heart in me."

Hebrews 11:6 "He rewards those who look to him."

Proverbs 3:6 "Remember the Lord in everything you d, and he will give you success" (NCV).

James 4:8 "Come near to God, and God will come near to you" (NCV).

Princess Power — It's your turn!

★ Make a Valentine for Jesus, telling Him how much you love Him. Use construction paper, glitter, paper doilies, and glue.

★ Read your Bible a little each day, and write love notes to God in a pretty journal or diary.

Love Note: Princess, as you spend time with God in His Word, think about what He is saying to you personally.

★ Using 8 inches of satin ribbon and ¼ inch plastic pony beads, make a bookmark for your journal. Make another one for your Bible, to mark where you are reading. Remember that even young girls can read a couple of verses in the Bible each day. ***(You can set a time to read your Bibles together.)***

Dear Jesus,

Thank You for loving me with a forever love.
Thank You for creating me and delighting in
me. I love You, Lord, and I want to seek You
with all my heart. Help me to want to learn
more about You, and to show others my devotion
to You.

In Jesus's name, I pray. Amen.

Princess Pledge

I promise to

Princess Choice 6 —

Security:
Knowing God's Love

Dear Mom: This Tiara Truth of security will focus on being secure in the Father's love. Your daughter will begin to understand that Jesus is always with her and watching over her. All women struggle with becoming secure "in their own skin." This is a chance to begin exposing your daughter to the wonderful facts that she is "fearfully and wonderfully made" (Psalm 139:14 NIV), and the Father who designed her keeps His eyes on His masterpiece — daily. We moms need to know and remember that part of Jesus's prayer for us in the garden was asking the Father to keep an "eye on us." (See John 17:11–12.) Talk about security!

Message to Mom

> "All that I am, or hope to be, I owe to my angel mother."
> —Abraham Lincoln

77

Tiara Truth — Security

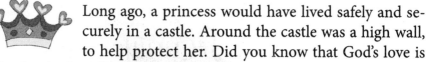

Long ago, a princess would have lived safely and securely in a castle. Around the castle was a high wall, to help protect her. Did you know that God's love is like that high wall of protection around the castle? No matter what happens, a princess can be safe and secure in God's love that surrounds her even better than a castle wall.

God wants us to be secure in His love. He wants us to rest safe and sound in His security blanket of love. I'm so glad that Jesus is always with us in times of trouble. He is there to comfort us when we fall. So Princess, when Jesus says "Come," you can say, "Look out Jesus, here I come!"

"No good thing does he withhold from those whose walk is blameless" (Psalm 84:11).

Here I Come

There once was a little girl named Kara who had big beautiful eyes and shiny brown curls. She wasn't much more than a baby, just learning how to walk. Can you imagine what happened after she took a few steps? You guessed correctly! She fell down with a big *kerplop (Pat your feet.)* and started to cry *(Rub your eyes.)*.

Her rosy cheeks turned wet from the puddles of water that formed in her big eyes, and tears flowed down her face. Her mommy called her name, and with arms opened wide, invited the little one to come into mommy's arms. *(Open wide your arms.)* But do you know what the little girl did? She just sat in the middle of the floor and cried all the more.

The mom was very sad *(frown)*. Mom knew, if her child would come to her, that she would hold her child in her lap. She would wrap her arms around her and kiss away her tears. *(Wrap your arms around your daughter, set her in your lap, and kiss her cheeks.)* The mommy wanted to comfort her precious little girl, so she continued to call her name.

Finally, Kara crawled over to her mommy and climbed into her mother's lap. I bet you know what happened next! The little one stopped crying, because she was no longer afraid. Kara knew she was now safe and secure with her mom.

And do you know what? That is exactly what Jesus wants us to do.

Princess Portrait — A Little Slave Girl —
Kidnapped but Secure in Her God

"Now bands from Aram had gone out and had taken captive a young girl from Israel, and she served Naaman's wife. She said to her mistress, 'If only my master would see the prophet who is in Samaria! He would cure him of his leprosy'" (2 KINGS 5:2–3 NIV).

A little girl was kidnapped and taken far away from her family. She lost everything dear to her. But she behaved so bravely. She became a maid, and one day she told the woman she served that she believed God could heal the woman's husband, who was terribly sick. Is that not amazing? A little girl so secure in the God she loved that she spoke proudly of His power!

This young girl's tears had stopped after her kidnapping! Her faith in God was still strong. Her dad and mom must have taught her that even if she were away from her parents, her heavenly Father would be with her always.

So a very sick man was healed, because a little kidnapped girl was secure in her God.

Ruth 1:16 "But Ruth replied, 'Don't try to make me leave you and go back. Where you go I'll go. Where you stay I'll stay. Your people will be my people. Your God will be my God.'"(Ruth followed God all the way to Bethlehem, a long way from family and friends.)

Colossians 3:2 "Set your minds on things above, not on earthly things" (NIV).

Psalm 37:3–7 "Trust in the Lord and do good, dwell in the land and enjoy safe pasture. Delight yourself in the Lord and he will give you the desires of your heart. Commit your way to the Lord; trust in him and he will do this: He will make your righteousness shine like the dawn, the justice of your cause like the noonday sun. Be still before the Lord and wait patiently for him" (NIV).

Luke 12:34 "Where your treasure is, there your heart will be also" (NIV).

Proverbs 1:33a "Whoever listens to me will live in safety" (NIV).

Jeremiah 29:11 "I know the plans I have for you," announces the Lord. "I want you to enjoy success. I do not plan to harm you. I will give you hope for the years to come."

Psalm 84:11 "He doesn't hold back anything good from those whose lives are without blame."

Princess Power — It's your turn!

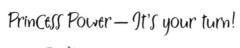

★ What is important to you? Cut out pictures of things that are important to you, like clothes, toys, and other things. Glue these pictures to construction paper. Put a big X over the things that can break or will not last forever. Now, think about things that won't break or wear out (for example, your parents' love, God's love, and God's Word).

Love Note: Princess, remember that material things will never be as important as God's love.

★ Draw a picture of a great place to hide where no one can find you. Play "Hide and Seek" with your family. Remember you can never hide from God, because He is always watching over you.

Dear Jesus,

Help me to remember that You are always watching over me. Help me to remember that . . .

my "stuff" will never be as important as doing what pleases You. Thank You, Lord, that . . .

Your love and comfort can never be destroyed or taken away from me.

In Jesus's name, I pray. Amen.

Princess Pledge

I promise to

Contentment:
Being Satisfied

Dear Mom: This Tiara Truth of contentment will focus on being happy and content with what we have. Your daughter will begin to understand that we can be full of joy when we focus on praising the Lord and not on what we have or do not have. Our daughters need to see this virtue of contentment on display in our daily lives.

Message to Mom

Have our daughters heard us whining more than giving thanks for everything that happens to us? Whining is like anger squeezed through a tiny whole. Girls young and old whine when they are angry about not getting their way.

What you don't resolve in your heart,
you will reproduce in others.

Tiara Truth — Contentment

I have learned to be content no matter what happens to me. "I'm not saying that because I need anything. I have learned to be content no matter what happens to me" (PHILIPPIANS 4:11).

Princess, what do you do when you don't get what you want? Do you whine or throw a fit? Hey, Jesus has a better idea. The Bible teaches us, "Give thanks no matter happens" (1 Thessalonians 5:18). So be thankful!

One of God's top ten rules is, "You shall not covet" (Exodus 20:17 and Deuteronomy 5:21). That means not to want more and more. We need to be happy with what God gives us. Wanting more and more only makes us unhappy. Have you been unhappy this week because you didn't get what you wanted?

The Hamster Dance

I know a little girl named Kenna, and she is often heard saying, "You get what you get, and you don't whine a bit." She is learning to be content and happy with what she gets! So Princess, don't be fooled into loving things. The new outfit or toy that you have been dreaming about will soon wear out or break. Be thankful and satisfied with the things you have. "In everything give thanks" (1 Thessalonians 5:18 ASV). If we practice being thankful, our hearts will be happy!

God wants us to jump for joy in the Lord, spin around in delight for Him! *(You may want to let your daughter jump with you and spin about.)* Do you know what reminds me of "jumping for joy in the Lord?' The Hamster Dance! You might be wondering why I would think of a hamster. What does a hamster have to do with jumping for joy in the Lord? Do you know what a hamster looks like? Well, it is much cuter than a mouse, and often while playing in its cage, it starts to spin around. It does a little dance that has been called the "Hamster Dance." Did you know there is a verse in the Old Testament Book of Habakkuk that describes a dance like this? This Bible verse says, "Yet I will rejoice in the LORD, I will joy in the God of my salvation" (Habakkuk 3:18 NKJV). "Rejoice in the Lord" may mean to jump and spin around for joy and delight in the Lord. Sounds like the Hamster Dance!

One night Dede's grandchildren (Kara, Austin, and Kenna) were visiting, and when they heard the Disney song "Hamster Dance," they all began to cheer and spin and jump around to the music. Now whenever they come for a visit, they love to say, "Do you know what time it is?" Grandma Dede replies, "It's time for the hamster dance!"

Did you know that when we spin around in delight about God, we are not thinking about our problems? That's right, we can only be full of joy when we are focused (concentrating) on loving and praising the Lord. So let's start spinning around for joy in the Lord!

Love Note for Mom: Oh, how our heavenly Father wants us to demonstrate the same joyous confidence no matter what our circumstances might be! When we are "spinning around," rejoicing and praising the Lord, we won't be able to focus on our problems! Our focus can only be on the Lord when we praise Him! So let's start spinning around for joy in the Lord! Mom, do you know what time it is? *It's time for the hamster dance!*

Did you know that whining can ruin a pretty face? Whining makes a princess forfeit (give up) her crown. Sounds like it's time for a "Tiara Time Out."

Moses's brave sister Miriam watched him as he floated down the Nile River. She watched the basket float right up to a great palace. Young Miriam bravely approached the king's daughter, who took Moses out of the river. Miriam offered to help with the baby who had been discovered in the basket (her little brother).

Read Exodus 2:4–8. It was this princess Miriam who had been hiding her little brother Moses from the Egyptians. They wanted to kill all the baby boys among God's chosen people, the Hebrews (or Israelites). Miriam helped save Moses, who grew up and many years later led millions of Israelites across the Red Sea. Miriam grew up, too, and became a leader in song.

Years later, Miriam wasn't singing and she wasn't helping her brother Moses any more. In fact, she was whining and complaining against Moses, and you won't believe what happened! She broke out with a disease, something far worse than zits or pimples; she had leprosy for a week. Do you ever whine when you don't get your way? When Jackie's little girl Jessi would whine, Jackie would put her fingers in her ears and say, "When you whine I can't hear you." *(Put fingers in your ears.)* Whining means that you think God is not enough. God's little princesses should not think that way.

Princess Pearls

This is a time for mother and daughter to "string a beautiful necklace" — together look up and study the pearls of wisdom found in God's Word. May the precious pearls of God's Word transform your daughter's heart into the heart of a princess!

Ruth 2:2 "And Ruth the Moabitess said to Naomi, "Let me go to the fields and pick up the leftover grain behind anyone in whose eyes I find favor." *Ruth did not complain when she had to work picking up leftovers in the field.*

Exodus 20:17 "Do not long for anything that belongs to your neighbor."

Colossians 3:15 "Let the peace that Christ gives rule in your hearts."

1 Thessalonians 5:16–17 "Always be joyful. Never stop praying."

Romans 1:21 "They knew God. But they didn't honor him as God. They didn't thank him."

Psalm 55:22 "Turn your worries over to the Lord. He will keep you going."

Philippians 4:11 "I'm not saying that because I need anything. I have learned to be content no matter what happens to me."

Psalm 73:25–26 "Whom have I in heaven but you? And earth has nothing I desire besides you. My flesh and my heart may fail, but God is the strength of my heart and my portion forever" (NIV).

James 4:1–2 "What causes fights and quarrels among you? Don't they come from your desires that battle within you? You want something but don't get it" (NIV).

Love Note: Discuss the Bible words with your little princess to see how God is transforming and strengthening her heart.

Princess Power — It's your turn!

★ Using poster board, markers, glitter, and streamers, make a "No Whiners Club" poster to hang in your room. Princess, be a member of the "No Whiners Club."

★ Treasure or Trap: Draw a picture of everything you are thankful for; this is your treasure. The trap is wanting more and more!

★ Play flashlight tag after dark. The person who is "it" must tag others by shining the flashlight on them. Think about how you can "shine your light for Jesus."

★ A to Z Thankfulness: Sit in a circle with friends and family. The first person says something she is thankful for, beginning with the letter A. For example, "Thank you, Lord, for angels watching over me." The next person gives thanks using the letter B. "Thank You, Lord, for bluebirds." The game continues through Z.

★ Write your name in the center of a piece of construction paper with a glue stick and sprinkle glitter over your name. When you are content and happy with what you have, YOU SHINE FOR JESUS!

Love Note: Decide to be happy when something good happens to those around you, and to share your blessings with others.

Princess Prayer

Dear Jesus,

Help me not to be a whiner. Help me to remember that Jesus is my true treasure, and I should be grateful for what I have been given. Help me break my whining habit.

In Jesus's name, I pray. Amen.

Princess Pledge

I promise to ~~~~~~~~~~~~~~~~~~~~~~~~~~~

~~~~~~

~~~~~~

~~~~~~

~~~~~~

~~~~~~

~~~~~~

~~~~~~

~~~~~~

~~~~~~

~~~~~~

Patience:
Waiting Without Whining

*D*ear Mom: This Tiara Truth of patience will focus on how patience protects us from hurtful consequences. Your daughter will begin to understand that when one chooses patience, life is more enjoyable. Does your princess see her mom being patient with the often chaotic aspects of her life? Does your daughter see you patiently standing in line in the grocery store? Mom, we can wear ourselves out trying to control and tame a tameless world. In fact, sometimes we become impatient with the pace of our own children. Is one of your children not behaving in school as you expected? We must try hard to remember that our children often provide opportunities for God-given "tutorials" for our spiritual growth.

Message to Mom

> We must accept our children where they are,
> and pray passionately for where they need to be.

Tiara Truth — Patience

"Be still. Be patient. Wait for the Lord to act"
(Psalm 37:7).

Think of patience as a beautiful pearl. Did you know that it takes a long time for a pearl to form? It forms inside an oyster shell because of something that is trapped inside. Whatever is trapped irritates or troubles the little animal that uses the shell as its house. The sea animal, the oyster, keeps making a covering over the itch—until a pearl forms! ***(Show your daughter an oyster shell and a pearl or string of pearls.)***

The pearl reminds us that something beautiful happens when we are patient. Just like a beautiful pearl is created inside an oyster over time, we have a beautiful heart when we are patient. You can have a kind heart just like a little girl I know, named Kara. When Princess Kara has friends come over to play, she invites them to become members of her "kindness club." The friends encourage one another to use kind words as they play in their clubhouse. It's so very hard for little girls to be kind unless they are being patient with one another. Remember Princess, patience give us the strength to be kind!

"Be still. Be patient. Wait for the Lord to act."

"Don't Spoil the Surprise"

When Dede was a little girl, her mommy planned a wonderful surprise for her. The gifts were hidden until Dede's special day. Well, one morning while Dede was playing, she discovered her gifts! At first Dede paused. She didn't want to spoil the surprise. But her impatient heart got the best of her. And do you know what Dede did? You guessed it, she was impatient and couldn't wait.

First, one box was opened, and then another, and another, until Dede had peeked inside every box! *(Act as though you are peeking inside boxes or actually do so with several empty boxes.)* Why is waiting so hard? Why is it so easy to lose patience? When the party began, Dede already knew what was in every gift box. How sad! The surprise was ruined. The consequence of her impatience was that there was now no joy in the surprise!

Princess, we must choose to wait patiently for God's best. Patience makes life easier and more enjoyable. Dede would have had more joy at her party if she had been patient. Patience helps us while we wait for things we are eager for, like our own birthday parties and when we celebrate Jesus's birthday, Christmas! We should not let our impatient feelings rob us of the special surprises God has for us.

Princess Portrait — Abigail

Princesses should encourage each other to be patient and kind. Some girls at school and even at church might not be kind. But when a girl has the heart of a princess, she can be kind when others aren't.

In 1 Samuel 25, there is a story about a beautiful woman named Abigail who was married to a very mean man. One day Abigail's patient kindness saved the lives of all the men who worked on her husband's ranch. Her patient kindness protected not only her life but the lives of others. Your patient kindness guards not only you but those around you too. In Hebrew language, the name *Abigail* means "a father's joy." When we are behaving wisely and choosing to be patient, we bring the heavenly Father joy. The Holy Spirit, our Helper, gives us the power to act wisely. Remember, patience is a fruit of the Spirit. When we make choices that show patience in our heart, we bring joy to the heavenly Father.

And this is true for how we behave at home, at school, and even church — you can choose to be like Abigail, who was patient and loving even when those around her were not wise or kind. Abigail learned as a young girl how to bring joy to the Father's heart.

Princess Pearls

This is a time for mother and daughter to "string a beautiful necklace" and study the pearls of wisdom found in God's Word.

Ruth 3:18 "Then Naomi said, 'Wait, my daughter, until you find out what happens. For the man will not rest until the matter is settled today" (NIV). Ruth chose to be patient.

Psalm 27:14 "Wait for the Lord. Be strong and don't lose hope. Wait for the Lord."

Proverbs 3:5–6 "Trust in the Lord with all your heart, and lean not on your own understanding; in all you ways acknowledge him, and he will make your paths straight" (NIV).

Psalm 37:7 "Rest in the Lord and wait patiently for Him" (KJV).

Romans 5:3 "We are full of joy even when we suffer. We know that our suffering gives us the strength to go on."

Princess Power — It's your turn!

★ Draw a picture of a time when you had to wait patiently.

Love Note: Princess, think of a time you didn't wait patiently. Tell Mom about the consequences of your impatience.

★ Mom-and-Me Time: Fill a pot with potting soil. Plant some flower seeds with mom's help. Keep the soil moist. Place the pot in a sunny spot. Now wait and see what happens. Watch it blossom and grow.

Love Note: Princess, just like a seed may take a while to grow and bloom into a flower, God's plan for your life may take some time. Don't be impatient, God has a wonderful plan for you and He will make it happen. You will blossom and bloom for Jesus!

★ Mom-and-Me Time: Make a package of fruit-flavored gelatin. Follow the directions on the box, except don't wait for the gelatin to gel. What happens when you take the gelatin out of the fridge too soon? Make a list of things you are waiting for. What happens if you are impatient? Make a choice to wait with calmness, self-control, and no whining. Now that's patience!

Princess Prayer

Dear Jesus,

Sometimes it's hard for me to wait. Please help me to be patient and trust You as I wait for Your perfect plan for my life. I love You, Lord!

In Jesus's name, I pray. Amen!

Princess Pledge

I promise to ~~~~~~

~~~~~~

~~~~~~

~~~~~~

~~~~~~

~~~~~~

~~~~~~

~~~~~~

~~~~~~

~~~~~~

~~~~~~

Prepared for Her Prince:
Keeping Jesus Number One

*D*ear Mom: This Tiara Truth will focus on the best that God has **Message** for His princesses, whom He may call to marriage someday **to Mom** to a prince of a man — a Boaz — not a Bozo. Or God may become your daughter's husband, and you want her prepared for a wonderful, joy-filled life with Him as her all and all.

Nevertheless, mentoring your daughter in the God-honoring choices of this book will help her grow into God's best, whether she marries or not. If she does marry, it will help her to focus on her love relationship with God first and be prepared for Mr. Right. Daily, our girls are exposed to messages that prepare even little girls to attract a Bozo guy rather than God's best. This book is also a beginner's guidebook to a Boaz; *not a Bozo*! Remember, Mom, the most important decision of our daughters' lives will be covered in the next lesson — Jesus as her Master, and the second most important decision of her life, who will possibly be her Mr.

Learn to wait for God's best, and avoid a Bozo in a life mate.

Tiara Truth — Choosing God's Best (Conviction)

 Choosing God's best is possible for a girl with the heart of a princess. With the heart of a princess, you will be wise enough to make good choices, and others will see your princess heart in action. (See Ruth 3:11.)

When a little girl develops the heart of a princess, she will love God first, with all of her heart. And she may someday want to love a young man who has the heart of a prince. She needs to learn while she is young that God may very well have a prince for her to waltz with someday — a prince who learned the principles that a heart of a princess has learned.

There once was a prince named Amnon, and his name meant "trustworthy," but sadly, he did not live up to his name. He was selfish and unkind and hurt another princess very deeply. You know what a perfect name would be for a hurtful prince? Instead of Prince Charming, he should be called Prince Harming! God wants to protect His princesses from being hurt by "Prince Harming."

There is a prince of a man in the Bible whose name was Boaz. Every girl with the heart of a princess needs to pray for her "Boaz." Every girl can pray that her prince of a man will learn the same kind of "tiara truths" that she has learned.

Kim's Precious Pocket List

Jackie has a niece who, throughout her teen years, would carry in her wallet a precious pocket list. *(Prepare a short list of the words that represent good princess choices, from this book, and have it in your pocket.)* What was on this list? It was a list of qualities that she was looking for in a "future" boyfriend and eventually a husband. *(Pull out your list and read.)*

Whenever a boy would ask her for a date, she would think about her "pocket list." And if the boy was not making good choices as a prince should, she would say no to his invitations for a date. *(Shake your head a moment and fold your arms closed.)*

Kim's precious pocket list kept her from dating Prince Harming (Mr. Bozo), which made not only God happy but also her parents. *(Smile and nod your head.)*

Princess Portrait — Ruth

Ruth and Naomi returned to Bethlehem. There Ruth decided that she should go to find food. It was harvest time, so Ruth went to work in the fields, following harvesters and picking up any grain they dropped. The owner of the fields, Boaz, came by to greet the harvesters and saw Ruth. Boaz believed in God and was kind. Boaz asked one of his men who she was. The man replied, "She came from Moab with Naomi. She has been hard at work all morning."

Boaz went to Ruth. He said, "Don't go work in any other field. Stay here with the other servant girls. I will make sure you are safe. When you are thirsty, go and get a drink from the water jar." Boaz told his men not to bother Ruth. Ruth bowed down to Boaz and asked, "Why are you being so nice to me? I am a stranger here." Boaz replied, "I know what you've done for Naomi. I have seen your kind deeds." Ruth won Boaz's heart, through her loving behavior. Ruth thanked Boaz and then worked more in the hot sun. Boaz even ordered his workers to drop extra barley so Ruth could have more for herself.

Ruth took all the grain home and shared with Naomi, and told her that she had met Boaz. Later, Boaz married Ruth, and God blessed them with a baby boy, who they named Obed. Naomi was very happy. Obed became grandfather of the future king of Israel, David.

And so this is the true story of a girl named Ruth, who left everything she had known to trust in the one true God. (Adapted from Ruth 2.)

Love Note: Read the sweet love story of Boaz and Ruth (Ruth 2–3). See if you can find the heart of a princess in Ruth. Was Ruth kind and willing to help others? Or was Ruth selfish? Was Ruth patient? Have you read about her faith?

Princess Pearls

These Scriptures help your daughter understand that God has the best for His princesses.

Ruth 3:11 "I will do for you all you ask. All my fellow townsmen know that you are a woman of noble character" (NIV).

Romans 8:28 "We know that in all things God works for the good of those who love him."

Joshua 24:15 "Choose for yourselves this day whom you will serve" (NIV).

Psalm 84:11 "No good thing does He withhold from those whose walk is blameless" (NIV).

Princess Power — It's Your Turn!

★ Mom-and-Me Time: Paint a T-shirt using fabric paint. Paint the phrase: No Bozo, Only Boaz

Love Note: One of the grown-up ladies who made this book has a daughter named Jessi. Jessi slept in a NO BOZO T-shirt as a little girl. This was a constant reminder of the Prince Harming to avoid. Jessi is now married to a man with the heart of a prince — a Boaz.

Princess Prayer

Dear Jesus,

I know I am too young to be worried about the man I will marry someday, but today I want to pray that I will never marry anyone that doesn't have the heart of a prince of God.

Amen.

(NO BOZO)

Princess Choice 9 – Prepared for Her Prince

Princess Pledge

I promise to ~~~~~~~~~~~~~~~~~~~~~~~~~~~~~~~~

~~~~~~

~~~~~~

~~~~~~

~~~~~~

~~~~~~

~~~~~~

~~~~~~

~~~~~~

~~~~~~

Love Note to Mom: Reviewing these lessons as she grows will help your princess waltz gracefully with the King of kings for a lifetime, displaying the heart of a princess!

A Royal Heart:
Receiving Salvation

*D*ear Mom: This is the most important Tiara Truth to share with your daughter. This is a special opportunity for you to share with your daughter about God's most precious gift to her heart: Jesus! If your daughter expresses to you a desire to ask Jesus to forgive her of her sins, share the ABCs of salvation. Pray with her as she makes the most important decision of her life.

Message to Mom

Mom, remember that eternity is too long to be wrong. May this encourage your boldness to share Jesus not only with your child but also with those your children will bring into your life. Please read the ABCs, even if your daughter is born again. This is an opportunity for your daughter to review with you how to share her faith with others.

Tiara Truth — The Choice of a Royal Heart — (Receiving Salvation)

 Will you give your heart to Jesus? When you give your heart to Jesus, He changes your heart, and makes you brand-new inside. This is the most important Tiara Truth, princess. This is a special opportunity for you to receive God's most precious gift to your heart, Jesus!

Celebrate with the Angels

Jackie's family had a tradition of "celebrating with the angels" (Luke 15:10). Whenever a family member helped someone to know Jesus, they would have a "Celebrate with the Angels" meal. They were celebrating with the angels in heaven that rejoice whenever someone is born again; when someone becomes part of God's royal family. They would place a porcelain angel at the center of the table, with two candles on each side. They would light the candles and serve a special dessert by candlelight. Then they said the names of the people who had invited Jesus to be their Savior.

Jackie told her children, Ben and Jessica, that their prayers had helped. Nine-year-old Jessica had the privilege of helping to lead a classmate to know Jesus. Jackie rejoiced with Jessica and commended her courage to share God's simple plan of salvation. And they held another "Celebrate with the Angels" family time. Jackie asked Jessica what type of dessert she might enjoy during this special family time. Jessica responded, "Mom, would it be OK if we celebrate with the angels at Bud's Chicken?" Jackie laughed and assured Jessica that they could celebrate with the angels anywhere!

A Royal Heart

God is the King of the universe, and when you give your heart to Jesus, you become a child of God. Since God is King, that makes you His princess. (See John 1:12.)

You have the privilege of asking Jesus to forgive you of your wrongdoing or sins, using these ABC's of a Royal Heart — that's salvation.

When Jackie and Dede were young girls, they became a part of God's royal family. It's true! When you believe that Jesus died for your sins (any action, attitude, words, or thoughts that do not please God), you tell Jesus that you are sorry for the wrong things you have done. You ask Him to forgive you by believing in Him, and something wonderful happens. God gives you the gift of eternal life. That means you are a part of God's royal family, with a royal heart!

It's as easy as ABC . . . .

(Review this in advance and let it be a natural, conversational communication with your daughter, and be prepared to answer any questions she has or to help her get answers to her questions from a family member, church friend, or pastor.)

Love Note to Mom: the Princess Prayer on page 121 is a chance for you to lead your daughter in repeating the prayer of salvation.

A . . . Admit to God that I have sinned; that I have done wrong things.

Romans 3:23 "Everyone has sinned. No one measures up to God's glory."

B . . . Believe that Jesus loves me and died on the Cross for my sins.

John 3:16 "God loved the world so much that he gave his one and only Son. Anyone who believes in him will not die but will have eternal life."

C . . . Confess my sin (any action, attitude, words, or thoughts that do not please God) and receive Jesus.

1 John 1:9 "But God is faithful and fair. If we admit that we have sinned, he will forgive us our sins. He will forgive every wrong thing we have done. He will make us pure."

John 1:12 "Some people did accept him. They believed in his name. He gave them the right to become children of God."

John 3:16 God showed His love for us by sending His Son Jesus to earth.

Romans 3:23 But what is in our heart that keeps us from God? "Everyone has sinned."

(Review in advance.)

That's right! The problem is sin. Our hearts are unclean because of sin. Sin is disobeying God's rules. Can you think of some things that are sin *(disobeying parents, lying, being unkind)*? You're right! Sins are thoughts and actions that do not please God.

Sin keeps us apart from God. God cannot allow sin where He is. God loves us so much that He made a way for you and me to be forgiven. He sent His precious Son Jesus to die on the Cross for our sins. Jesus took your punishment and mine when He died on the Cross.

The Bible says, "But God is faithful and fair. If we admit that we have sinned, he will forgive us our sins. He will forgive every wrong thing we have done. He will make us pure" (1 John 1:9).

Would you like to belong to Him forever? All you have to do is agree with God that you have sinned and ask God to forgive you and make your heart clean. This is what we do when we believe in Christ; trusting in Christ for eternal life.

Princess Portrait — Ruth

Ruth came from a background that did not worship the one true God. As a little girl, she worshiped a false or fake god. Then, through the example of a loving older woman, Naomi, Ruth was introduced to the one true God. (See Ruth 1:16).

(Tell your princess): **Little Lady in Waiting, you do not have to wait until you are all grown up to have a relationship with Jesus, to be His princess. Ruth didn't learn this truth as a little girl, but you don't have to wait until you are all grown up.** *You can trust in Jesus now!*

Princess Pearls

John 3:16 "God loved the world so much that he gave his one and only Son. Anyone who believes in him will not die but will have eternal life."

Romans 3:23 "Everyone has sinned. No one measures up to God's glory."

1 John 1:9 "But God is faithful and fair. If we admit that we have sinned, he will forgive us our sins. He will forgive every wrong thing we have done. He will make us pure."

Revelation 3:20 "Here I am! I stand at the door and knock. If any of you hears my voice and opens the door, I will come in and eat with you. And you will eat with me."

You can be born into God's family when you pray
something like this:

"Lord Jesus, I know I have sinned. I have
done wrong things. I believe You died on the
Cross for me and were punished for my sins.
Please forgive my sins and make my heart
Clean. I want to trust and follow You as my Lord
and Savior." In Jesus's name, I pray. Amen.

Princess Power — It's your turn!

★ Draw a self-portrait, and don't forget to put a tiara on your head!

★ Celebrate! It's your birthday; record your spiritual birthday in your Bible!

Love Note to Mom: Don't forget to celebrate your daughter's spiritual birthday in the coming years — make cupcakes to celebrate this special day!

What's the greatest news you have ever heard? Maybe your parents told you that you could finally have that puppy you'd been waiting for. Would you want to keep that news to yourself? NO! I bet you would want to tell all your friends! It's so hard to keep good new to yourself! Because you are a Christian now, you can tell your friends and family how you became a Christian. That's called your *testimony*. So, tell a friend about the love of Jesus. God wants all people to hear how they can be a part of His royal family.

★ Print a list of people or draw a picture of all the people you want to tell about Jesus.

★ On a 3-by-5-inch card, print your name, the month, day, and year when you became a Christian. Decorate the card using stickers and markers. When you finish, place the card in your treasure box.

Love Note: Remember, Princess, becoming a Christian is a once in a lifetime decision. No one can take it away from you.

★ Write a love note to Jesus, thanking Him for dying on the Cross for you and for giving you eternal life. Place your note in your treasure box.

When you ask Jesus to come into your heart, He gives you eternal life — He also gives you His Holy Spirit. Why is this so special? He is always with you, day and night, protecting, comforting, and guiding you. The Holy Spirit gives us the power each day to live the tiara truths and in ways that are found in Galatians 5:21–23:

Obedience
Diligence
Faith
Virtue
Devotion
Security
Contentment
Patience

"But the fruit the Holy Spirit produces is love, joy and peace. It is being patient, kind and good. It is being faithful and gentle and having control of oneself" (GALATIANS 5:22-23).

Princess Pledge

I promise to〜〜〜〜〜〜〜〜〜〜〜〜〜〜〜〜

〜〜〜〜〜〜〜〜〜〜〜〜〜〜〜〜〜〜

〜〜〜〜〜〜〜〜〜〜〜〜〜〜〜〜〜〜

〜〜〜〜〜〜〜〜〜〜〜〜〜〜〜〜〜〜

〜〜〜〜〜〜〜〜〜〜〜〜〜〜〜〜〜〜

〜〜〜〜〜〜〜〜〜〜〜〜〜〜〜〜〜〜

〜〜〜〜〜〜〜〜〜〜〜〜〜〜〜〜〜〜

〜〜〜〜〜〜〜〜〜〜〜〜〜〜〜〜〜〜

〜〜〜〜〜〜〜〜〜〜〜〜〜〜〜〜〜〜

〜〜〜〜〜〜〜〜〜〜〜〜〜〜〜〜〜〜

〜〜〜〜〜〜〜〜〜〜〜〜〜〜〜〜〜〜

Heart of a Princess Club

Mom-and-Me Time: Read this list and then add your name and a favorite Bible verse. Now, you are a member of the Heart of a Princess Club!

♥ Abigail — She was wise and generous. (1 Samuel 25)

♥ Anna — She waited on the Lord. (Luke 2)

♥ Deborah — She led in battle, bold and courageous! (Judges 4–5)

♥ Mary — She said, "Whatever, Lord!" (Matthew 1–2)

♥ Hagar — She trusted that God would take care of her. (Genesis 16)

♥ Elizabeth — Put her hope in the Lord. (Luke 1)

♥ Esther — She was a courageous beauty contest winner. (Esther 1–2)

♥ Miriam — She was Moses's courageous older sister. (Numbers 12)

♥ Ruth — This young woman was a loyal friend. (Ruth 1:16)

♥ Hannah — She prayed and was full of faith. (1 Samuel 2)

♥ Mary & Martha — One sister sat at Jesus's feet, the other served. (John 11–12)

♥ Huldah — She spoke God's message. (2 Chronicles 34:14–33)

♥ Lydia — She made purple cloth; was faith-full and followed Jesus. (Acts 16)

♥ Rebekah — She was kind, hardworking, and diligent. (Genesis 24–25)

- ♥ Princess Kim — Kara's mom (2 Chronicles 16:9)
- ♥ Princess Kelly — Kenna's mom (Psalm 119:10)
- ♥ Princess Jessica — Jackie's daughter (2 Timothy 1:7)
- ♥ Princess Dede — mentored (Romans 12)
  many little girls
- ♥ Princess Jackie — mentored (Isaiah 50:4)
  many older princesses

Add your name   **Your favorite Bible verse**

~~~~~~~~~~~~~~~~~~~~~~~~~~~~~~   ~~~~~~~~~~~~~~~~~~~~~~~~~~~~~~

Add more Bible names   **Favorite Bible verse**

~~~~~~~~~~~~~~~~~~~~~~~~~~~~~~   ~~~~~~~~~~~~~~~~~~~~~~~~~~~~~~

~~~~~~~~~~~~~~~~~~~~~~~~~~~~~~   ~~~~~~~~~~~~~~~~~~~~~~~~~~~~~~

Add friends' names   **Favorite Bible verse**

~~~~~~~~~~~~~~~~~~~~~~~~~~~~~~   ~~~~~~~~~~~~~~~~~~~~~~~~~~~~~~

~~~~~~~~~~~~~~~~~~~~~~~~~~~~~~   ~~~~~~~~~~~~~~~~~~~~~~~~~~~~~~

Add in your journal as many names as you want, today, tomorrow, and in the years to come as you grow up.

Bonus Content

Crafts

★ **Make a Tiara:** Check online for sites, such as http://www.instructables.com/id/Make-your-own-paper-tiara/

★ **Make a Princess Wand:** Attach a bow and ribbons to a straw with tape.

★ **Make a Princess Ring:** Thread a chenille or a ribbon through a colorful button. Gently twist or tie ends to form a small ring that fits. (Don't twist too tightly!)

Princess Recognition

★ Add award stickers to a calendar for activities your daughter completes. Choose a time for a special yet simple celebration to acknowledge your princess. *Message to Mom*

★ **Write your princess a love letter:** Choose pretty stationery for a keepsake letter. Envelop and seal to this book's inside back cover. *Message to Mom*

Bible References

★ You'll find pretty *Princess Bible* resources online and at Christian bookstores.

New Hope® Publishers is a division of WMU®, an international organization that challenges Christian believers to understand and be radically involved in God's mission. For more information about WMU, go to www.wmu.com. More information about New Hope books may be found at www.newhopepublishers.com. New Hope books may be purchased at your local bookstore.

Other New Hope
Parenting Resources

The Mentoring Mom
11 Ways to Model Christ
for Your Child
Jackie Kendall
ISBN-10: 1-59669-005-4
ISBN-13: 978-1-59669-005-9

Missions Moments 2
52 Easy-to-Use Missional Messages
and Activities for Today's Family
Mitzi Eaker
ISBN-10: 1-59669-210-3
ISBN-13: 978-1-59669-210-7

Mommy Pick-Me-Ups
Refreshing Stories
to Lighten Your Load
Edna Ellison and Linda Gilde
ISBN-10: 1-59669-218-9
ISBN-13: 978-1-59669-218-3

Available in bookstores everywhere.

For information about these books or any New Hope product, visit www.newhopepublishers.com.